THE POCKET MANIFEST DREAMS

Published in 2025
by Gemini Books
Part of Gemini Books Group

Based in Woodbridge and London

Marine House, Tide Mill Way
Woodbridge, Suffolk IP12 1AP
United Kingdom
www.geminibooks.com

Text and Design © 2025 Gemini Adult Books Ltd
Part of the Gemini Pockets series

Cover image: Unsplash/Chuttersnap (star) and /Sindy Süßengut (hand)
Text by Becky Freeth
Design by Jenny Semple

ISBN 978-1-78675-180-5

All rights reserved. No part of this publication may be reproduced in any form or by any means – electronic, mechanical, photocopying, recording or otherwise – or stored in any retrieval system of any nature without prior written permission from the copyright holders.

A CIP catalogue record for this book is available from the British Library.

Disclaimer: The book is a guidebook purely for information and entertainment purposes only. All trademarks, individual and company names, brand names, registered names, quotations, celebrity names, logos, dialogues and catchphrases used or cited in this book are the property of their respective owners. The publisher does not assume and hereby disclaims any liability to any party for any loss, damage or disruption caused by errors or omissions, whether such errors or omissions result from negligence, accident or any other cause. This book is an unofficial and unauthorized publication by Gemini Adult Books Ltd and has not been licensed, approved, sponsored or endorsed by any person or entity.

Printed in China

10 9 8 7 6 5 4 3 2 1

THE POCKET

MANIFEST DREAMS

Achieve your best life through positivity

G:

CONTENTS

Introduction — 6

CHAPTER ONE
Asking the Universe — 8

CHAPTER TWO
Manifesting the Material — 54

CHAPTER THREE
Love & Relationships — 78

CHAPTER FOUR
Healing & Emotions — 100

Conclusion & Credits — 124

Introduction

Do you dream of a new career? A bigger house? Meeting your soulmate? No matter how big you dream, manifestation could help you make it a reality. It is the practice of transforming positive thoughts into positive outcomes with a clear vision, purposeful actions and firm, unwavering belief in the power of the universe. Put simply, it is about "thinking" your dream life into existence.

Since ancient times, humans have written about the power of the mind in controlling our external state. Modern spiritual leaders believe that whether it's health or wealth, love or success you seek, you can attract it with your thoughts and actions. Raising vibrations

So, what do you really want?
The universe is listening.

Chapter One

ASKING THE UNIVERSE

MANIFEST DREAMS

In its simplest form, to manifest is to make something materialize. But how does it work? First, you need to know the tools and how to use them in the most effective way. It all starts with giving off the right energy and how we act like magnets for our dreams.

> **"Success attracts success and failure attracts failure because of the law of harmonious attraction."**

Napoleon Hill, *Succeed and Grow Rich through Persuasion* (1989)

The law of attraction

Everything in the universe is made up of energy: from the human body to the cup of tea in your hands. Even your thoughts, emotions and feelings. There are certain laws that govern our universe but manifestation was founded on the idea that "like attracts like" when it comes to your thoughts. Positive thoughts attract positive outcomes as negativity draws more negativity. Think of it like you might gravitate towards a smiling stranger when you're in a happy mood, more than you might on a bad day.

ASKING THE UNIVERSE

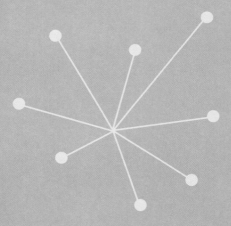

This is the Law of Attraction and in 2006, a famous book called *The Secret* asserted that thinking hard enough about your dreams sends a signal to the universe to magnetically attract "like" things. Money would therefore come to people who focus on wealth, rather than on debt.

MANIFEST DREAMS

By this "law", you attract whatever is in your mind: If you ask and believe, then you will receive. These days, manifestation leaders emphasize the importance of changing your behaviour in line with your thoughts to show that it is not a passive experience.

Rather, you are the conductor of the orchestra. The driver of the train. You determine the destination and the universe is the vehicle to get you there.

Raising vibrations

In manifestation, they say that you must become the energy you want to attract. Our energy moves on vibrations and we have the power to raise or lower them with our minds. High vibrations are associated with positive emotions, such as: contentment, calm, hope, confidence, love. Whereas low vibrations come in the form of negative emotions, like: fear, hate, guilt, jealousy, insecurity.

The process of manifestation is focused on elevating your energy in order to attract the same positivity. Visualizing the destination, positive thinking and setting intentions are all important tools associated with raising our vibrations.

MANIFEST DREAMS

Emotions = Energy

Your feelings can range from bad energy to good vibrations.

HIGH VIBES

LOVE
PEACE
HAPPINESS
GRATITUDE
KINDNESS
ENTHUSIASM
CONTENTMENT

APATHY
ANXIETY
DEPRESSION
JEALOUSY
FEAR
ANGER
SHAME

LOW VIBES

MANIFEST DREAMS

Visualization

Picturing your destination clearly and specifically is the first step in communicating what you want to the universe. It's about creating a vivid, visual experience in your mind (or on paper) about what you are trying to manifest in order to trigger the positive feelings and energy needed to attract it in real life.

ASKING THE UNIVERSE

The key to this is detail. How else will the universe know what you really want? For example, to visualize the new car you want, ask yourself:

✳ **What colour is it?**
✳ **What material are the seats?**
✳ **Where will I store my coffee or sunglasses?**

That way, you can really feel what it is like to have your dream car.

Visualize with the senses

Some people visualize well in their heads. They can successfully imagine objects, scenarios, details, even whole dialogues in their minds and replay them with vivid clarity. Others prefer visualization to take a more physical form by creating a vision board on paper that might feature fabrics, words, printed images or magazine cut-outs.

In any case, setting the scene helps. Certain music or scents facilitate the mental and physical space to dream like this and make it easier to tap into the same creative visions on a regular basis.

> **"Thoughts alone won't make extraordinary things happen. But nothing ever happens if you don't visualize it first."**

Lewis Pugh, *Yaks and a Speedo* (2013)

MANIFEST DREAMS

Positive thinking

Harnessing energy for positive outcomes
demands positive thoughts. Imagine the
universe can see your vision loud and clear, but
they are deafened by the sound of your negative
inner dialogue.

"I don't have any friends."
"I am stuck in this job and going nowhere."
"I don't have enough money for a new car."

Is that really what you want the
universe to hear?

ASKING THE UNIVERSE

Instead of focusing on what you don't have, thinking positively starts by drawing your attention to, and showing gratitude for, the abundance you do have in your life. Feelings of contentment, enthusiasm and joy are all associated with positive energy, whereas jealousy, resentment and sadness give off negative energy.

So, when we fixate on areas where we are lacking, we send our energy spiralling. Something as simple as thinking more positively provides a more hopeful narrative for your whole life.

MANIFEST DREAMS

Write it down

Getting your positive thoughts down on paper is a powerful exercise in paying attention, as well as replaying the high-energy feelings associated with them. For example, a gratitude list is a record of all the things in your life that make you proud, happy, thankful. Showing appreciation to the universe is like saying: "Thank you, I want more of this."

Journalling

Another helpful technique is a daily positivity journal where you diarize the uplifting experiences of your day from start to finish, showing equal appreciation for the smallest and mightiest achievements. This concentration on positivity and abundance raises your energy in order to attract it back to you.

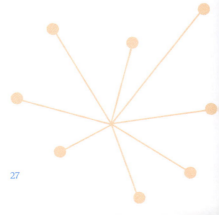

Affirmations

It's one thing to think a certain way but how do you come to believe that you are worthy of better things? Ultimately, what you say to yourself matters as much as what you say to others. When you replace the negative beliefs you have about yourself with positive, healing words or phrases, eventually your subconscious mind can start to reprogramme these statements as truths.

"I am worthless" ➤ "I am enough"

"I am weak" ➤ "I am strong"

"I don't matter" ➤ "I am capable"

We call these "affirmations" and they are a fundamental tool for manifestation. You can use them throughout the day, out loud, in your head or on paper. Sometimes reading affirmations has even more significance because the words can be visualized, too. The important thing is that they are repeated, over and over and over again until you deeply believe them.

MANIFEST DREAMS

Mantras

Usually associated with meditation and yoga practices, mantras are spiritual, often poetic-sounding phrases that you recite at times of deep, centred thought to help your mind deeply absorb them on a whole new level. An example might be:
"I have enough, I do enough, I am enough."

Try it, the universe is listening.

ASKING THE UNIVERSE

Manifestation mantras

Try repeating one of these mantras every morning when you wake up or during your bedtime routine.

❝I attract financial abundance into my life effortlessly.❞

❝I release any limiting beliefs about money and attract wealth into my life.❞

❝I am capable of giving myself the love and care I deserve.❞

❝I am beautiful, inside and out.❞

❝I am filled with energy, vitality and wellness.❞

❝I am strong and resilient, both physically and mentally.❞

Setting intentions

You would be mistaken for thinking that manifestation is a passive experience that "happens" to you. The moment you believe is when you start to achieve, because you will naturally change your behaviour patterns to suit your new reality and action is one aspect of manifestation that many people forget.

When you set intentions, you embody the person you aspire to be. Instead of talking about what you want like a far-off desire, you act it out in the here and now. Therefore, an Olympic hopeful might say to themselves: "I am a gold-medal winning athlete." An aspiring writer pitching to publishing houses should tell themselves, "I am a published author."

Suddenly, you treat yourself with the respect your dreams deserve and you subconsciously connect your desires with your behaviour.

MANIFEST DREAMS

Daily intention

Don't let the day dictate your mood – control
your positivity for the day and set yourself up
for success by repeating your intention.
Opposite are some examples:

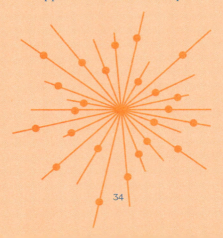

> "I will stay focused on my to-do list."

> "I will remind myself to enjoy the journey towards my goals."

> "I will be present in the moment and pay attention to what is around me."

MANIFEST DREAMS

The 369 numerology method

When it comes to intentions, it is not enough to "set it and forget it". Inventor Nikola Tesla believed that the key to powerful manifestation was repetition, because it shaped the actions taken to make them a reality. It is this consistency and commitment to your dreams that solidifies your purpose and direction.

Write down your intentions:
- ✷ 3 times in the morning.
- ✷ 6 times throughout the day.
- ✷ 9 times in the evening.

ASKING THE UNIVERSE

68 seconds to success

Certainly, you should manifest as often as possible to create change. But, does it matter how long you manifest for? According to Abraham-Hicks' teachings, it takes precisely 68 seconds to manifest effectively. The understanding is that you can shift your energy by focusing on a single "point of attraction" for 17 seconds.

No matter whether you are visualizing or repeating intentions, mantras and affirmations, this time must be uninterrupted for the law of attraction to kick in and start to attract thoughts and ideas on the same vibration that you have created.

Scripting

The next step is to act out those dreams in order to create a "lived" experience. Rather than writing about the here and now, learn how to write about the life you want as if you're already living it. Scripting is a practice that aims to convince your mind to think, feel and experience the emotions of your future self, therefore solidifying how rewarding it will feel to reach your goals.

You might write a letter to your former self, sharing wisdom about the future. The process is like creating a wise and reassuring older sibling who can help you place your limiting beliefs in the past.

Some people start a diary written by their future self, sharing (with specific detail) what it is really like to be the "you" of your dreams. Not only does it strengthen the actions you take towards this dream, but it blurs the lines between what is true and what is imagined in your mind.

Lunar manifesting

Aside from raising our vibrations from within, many people believe in harnessing the energy of our external environment for manifestation. Some fisherman and farmers observe the phases of the moon and how it affects the activity of fish and the rate of crop growth. But how does this relate to humans?

From earth, we observe a new moon every 29 days according to how it is lit by the sun. Within these cycles, we get phases of the moon that are said to turbo-charge the power of manifestation. A new moon represents new beginnings, and during the first half of the lunar cycle, it is believed that you can harness creative, proactive energy in setting intentions and making decisions. The energy shifts to a restful and reflective state at the time of a half moon, and we begin to tap into our emotions and gratitude.

To powerfully and effectively manifest, take full advantage of the fast, productive and reactive nature of the new moon.

MANIFEST DREAMS

MOON GUIDE

How do phases of the moon affect the way we manifest dreams?

NEW MOON
Set goals at this time of fresh, renewed perspective.

WAXING CRESCENT
Visualize and meditate during the creative window.

FIRST QUARTER
Apply strength and action to your intentions.

WAXING GIBBOUS
Focus. Show commitment to your goals in this new light.

FULL MOON
Channel the peak of your emotions and energy into creativity.

WANING GIBBOUS
Be open to new opportunities and show gratitude.

LAST QUARTER
Slow down and reflect on the goodness coming your way.

WANING CRESCENT
Time to let go. Release bad energy. Prepare for a new cycle.

Grounding yourself

Successful manifestation is as much about "timing" as it is about "priming" the mind and body. Grounding is the idea that you can increase the energy flow in your body by connecting more closely with the earth. Walking, lying or sitting on natural ground improves your skin-to-earth contact, therefore elevating your frequency by absorbing the natural energy source from the earth's surface.

Take your shoes off, step outside and practise your morning mantras with your skin touching the ground. Can you notice a difference?

ASKING THE UNIVERSE

Water manifesting

The same theory applied to grounding applies to water, which has long been highly regarded for its healing properties. Some people "anchor" their intentions by repeating positive affirmations whenever they are in contact with water.

Another well-known technique is a "spiritual bath". Immersing yourself in water, whether it is outdoors in nature or relaxing in the tub, can increase feelings of relaxation and peace, which are both associated with raised vibrations.

MANIFEST DREAMS

Grounding methods

Here are just a few of the ways you can prime yourself for manifestation.

1 Go Barefoot
In the park or woods, in your garden or on the beach, this simple action connects you immediately to the earth.

2 Body Scan
Lie down, relax your body and close your eyes. Starting with your head and working down to your feet, quietly check in with your body, noticing any aches and pains and any places where you are holding tension; release and relax that tension.

3 Balance Your Root Chakra
Known as Muladhara in Sanskrit, the root chakra is set at the base of the spine and represents stability and security. Using

meditation, yoga, visualization and crystals can help you attain balance in this chakra.

4 Breathing Meditation

Sit on the floor in a comfortable position, feeling the support of the ground beneath you. Take three deep, slow inhales and exhales, paying attention to your breathing.

Now calm your mind. Notice any thoughts that come into your head and let them pass by without dwelling on them.

Set an intention that the thoughts that didn't belong to you find a way back to where they do belong. If anxieties interrupt you, set an intention that the worry will turn to trust.

Keep breathing slowly. Thank the earth for its stability and the sky for its light.

Energy healing

Not many people consider that they could
be standing in the way of their own dreams.
Negative emotions like envy and anger are some
of the biggest blockers to manifestation because
they reinforce the negative flow of thoughts and
emotions that obstruct any hope we are trying
to send out for our lives.

ASKING THE UNIVERSE

You are worthy of what you want

To heal from this bad energy takes inner work using techniques like affirmations, mantras and positive thinking, which build up your own self-worth and belief that you are deserving of exactly what others have, or of what you so desperately want. Only then will it be possible to move ahead with your goals.

MANIFEST DREAMS

Sending out to the universe

To send out to the universe is to surrender your hopes to a higher power. When you ask for a clear and precise outcome, you have to be prepared to release it, replacing any fear or doubt about what comes next with unwavering positivity.

Again, that doesn't mean that you are passive in the process, but it means that you trust in it, even when you are faced with obstacles. Things might not change overnight. They might not even go the way you expected. But when you send and receive from the universe, you are always going in the right direction.

The work begins with (and always comes back to) the fundamentals you have learned about manifestation so far, and if you believe, then there should be no limit to where manifestation can take you!

Manifestation myths

"Thinking positively is enough."
Manifestation requires positive feeling and action too.

"If I ask, I will receive."
You play a leading part in making your goals happen.

"Your future is in the hands of the universe."
Manifestation is more like a partnership with the universe.

ASKING THE UNIVERSE

"You can manifest absolutely anything."
Sadly, winning the lottery is out
of your control.

"Manifestation is magic."
Actually no, but sometimes it might feel like it.

**"Challenges and setbacks mean
it's not working."**
Trust the process, you are on the right path.

Chapter Two

MANIFESTING THE MATERIAL

MANIFEST DREAMS

Is it wrong to want more? More money. More possessions. More opportunities. When it comes to manifestation, if you don't ask, then you don't get. Indeed, manifesting more for your life starts with being really honest about the things that will make you happy and fulfilled: whether it's cars, houses, clothes, fame or fortune. There's no shame here.

"Decide what you want. Believe you can have it. Believe you deserve it and believe it's possible for you. And then close your eyes and every day for several minutes, and visualize having what you already want, feeling the feelings of already having it."

Jack Canfield, author of *Chicken Soup for the Soul*, Facebook, 2012

MANIFEST DREAMS

More money

If you want to be a millionaire, first you have to act like one. People who want to manifest money talk about a wealth mindset where they harness the positive thoughts and purposeful daily habits of a millionaire in order to attract more fortune and opportunity.

For example, a millionaire does not ruminate on negative thoughts about themselves; they look at failures or setbacks as life lessons and push ahead. They focus on their goals with unwavering belief that they can and will achieve them, which programmes their subconscious to feel and act like a winner.

A millionaire takes incremental steps towards their goals, such as learning new skills; by seeing opportunities in everything, they put themselves in the right place to attract great outcomes, such as networking with colleagues or applying for high-level roles. A prosperous future is, therefore, no coincidence.

MANIFEST DREAMS

8 everyday actions of a millionaire

1 Get your 8 hours: Sleep aids performance and brain function.

2 Try new things: Open your mind to exciting opportunities.

3 Reach for the stars: Believe in yourself and your abilities.

4 Show gratitude: To attract money, you must focus on wealth.

5 Treat others: Giving encourages a "plentiful" mindset.

6 Pay yourself a compliment: What you tell yourself matters.

7 Feel good about money: You can be a money magnet.

8 Release resentment: It is how much you have in life that matters.

MANIFEST DREAMS

Freedom from debt

By the law of attraction, worrying about bills will only attract more financial strife. When you feel like you need money, you are more likely to have thoughts of lack and scarcity that will encourage an ongoing pattern of "need". Shift the balance to feelings of security or abundance and you can expect these things in return.

MANIFESTING THE MATERIAL

Wealth is a feeling

Ask yourself: What are the other areas of your life in which you feel "wealthy"? Think of the rich relationships you have with your parents, children, siblings, nieces or nephews. Make time for friendships that you value. Wear the outfit that makes you feel "a million dollars". Your life is already richer than you think.

> **"Your job is to declare what you would like to have from the catalogue of the universe. If cash is one of them, say how much you would like to have."**

Dr Joe Vitale,
The Attractor Factor (2005)

MANIFESTING THE MATERIAL

A new car

Whether you ask the universe for a Ferrari or a Ford, take positive actions as if you already own the car you want. If you dream of a state-of-the-art electric car, test drive it. Experience the thrill of a luxurious vehicle. Notice how other drivers on the road see you. Putting yourself in the driving seat will encourage you to act like the owner of the car. It suits you, doesn't it?

With that feeling in mind, go home and do the research. Decide where the electric charger port should be installed on your home. Price up the insurance. List your old car online. For every day afterwards, recall what it felt like to drive your dream car – it will reinforce your intentions and drive you towards that goal with small intentional changes, such as saving up when you want to be splashing out or working harder for that promotion even if you feel like giving up.

MANIFEST DREAMS

A dream home

Start a vision board for your dream house. Imagine the colours, textures and style of your future home to create a vivid experience of living there. Have fun with it. Experiment. Dream big. It's your vision board and something you might choose to share or keep private. Either way, draw your attention back to the board daily to reinforce that "lived" experience in your mind.

Sometimes marking a date on your vision board gives you a timeline to focus on. However, be mindful that house-hunting is a process with inevitable ups and downs. What's important is that you resist the temptation to give up on your dreams. Release frustration. Keep dreaming. The path may have changed direction, but it hasn't reached a dead end.

> **"To manifest, we have to first understand that we are the curators, the architects and the conductors of our lives and our destiny."**

Roxie Nafousi, *Manifest* (2022)

Career success

Everybody's definition of success is different, so you have the power to determine what that looks like to you. If you value the respect and recognition of your colleagues, the success of a forthcoming presentation might be your aim.

Visualize the moment of elation when your work is complete: a round of applause from the room, the high praise that follows, perhaps a surprise email to congratulate you.

Focus on those feelings of pride and relief. Let them drive the outcome of your presentation, rather than the anxiety, fear or doubt that could stand in your way of success.

MANIFEST DREAMS

Financial success

Success might mean a promotion or a pay rise to you. Exercising daily gratitude for the life you have right now will enable you to step into future success seamlessly, as if you have already welcomed your new job status.

This could come in the form of lists. Show appreciation for your strengths at work, for the life your job allows you to live and for the accomplishments you have achieved so far. You are consciously reinforcing why you deserve that next step.

MANIFESTING THE MATERIAL

Ways to manifest abundance

Believe in your ability, both to attract money and to take action towards your financial goals. Notice the potential for wealth creation that the universe offers, rather than the things that take money away from you.

1 Define your goals: How much money exactly do you want to attract and when? Write it down.

2 Repeat an affirmation: "I am open and ready to receive financial abundance." "Money flows to me freely and frequently."

3 Notice the angel number 888, which is associated with prosperity. Seeing it may indicate money is on its way.

4 Carry crystals, such as citrine, pyrite, green aventurine and jade, which are known for attracting wealth.

Career change visualization

A goal as lofty as a complete career change could seem like years ahead of you, but your enthusiasm for that goal will transform any resentment you experience within your current lifestyle that could be holding you back.

Script an ideal working day in the present tense, as if you have started your dream job. Be as detailed as possible, considering all of your senses as if you are experiencing it in real time.

MANIFESTING THE MATERIAL

Maybe the workplace you always dreamed of is a stylish yoga studio with floor-to-ceiling windows that flood the room with natural light and with views of a peaceful garden outside. Imagine the simmering feeling of nervous excitement when you arrive for your first class of the day.

You pop a window open, take a few energizing breaths of morning air and feel comforted by the sound of birds above. Take a moment to inhale the fresh peppermint as you enjoy a hot sip of herbal tea. Your first client arrives with the biggest smile on their face. You are exactly where you want to be.

> **"The visible is always a mirror of the invisible. The reality is imagined before it manifests itself."**

Paulo Coelho, author of *The Alchemist*, Facebook, 2010

MANIFESTING THE MATERIAL

Dreaming of travel

Do you spend your days dreaming about far-flung locations? You want to go backpacking in undiscovered territories. Or you'd rather sip exotic drinks in a turquoise paradise you can only reach by sea plane. Yet, here you are, telling yourself: "That is never gonna happen." Until you believe in infinite possibilities, the same really is true.

MANIFEST DREAMS

Moon manifesting for travel

Let's say you set yourself a month to change your energy. Harness the lunar cycles for powerful manifestation, starting on the day of a new moon. This is your decision-making phase and the best chance to set clear intentions about where you will go and how much you need to save. Promise it to yourself, and by the time the waxing crescent presents itself, you will be ready to communicate it to the universe through a creative vision board or clear thoughts in your head. Feel the excitement!

As the month progresses, fuel your next steps with the positive energy you have accumulated. For example, if you enter a competition for a trip, do so with the truest belief that you will win. Buy a guidebook and really imagine the moment you touch down at your dream destination.

The new moon, when energy and emotions peak, is the optimum time to clear space in your diary and start a savings pot. As your vibrations shift to reflection, look out for positive signs from the universe that you are attracting your dream, such as a travel article in your favourite magazine featuring the hotel from your vision board or a limited-time offer on the flights you've been researching.

Release any travel anxiety at this stage to make way for gratitude about what is to come.
You are making it happen!

Chapter Three

LOVE & RELATIONSHIPS

MANIFEST DREAMS

To manifest more love in your life, you have to know what it feels like first. From making friends or finding romance to healing rifts, you should be living, breathing and sleeping romance to shift your vibrations in the pursuit of love.
First step? Go and love yourself.

LOVE & RELATIONSHIPS

"Do not feel lonely, the entire universe is inside you. Stop acting so small. You are the universe in ecstatic motion. Set your life on fire."

Rumi

Making new friends

Putting yourself out there is uncomfortable. Whether you're motivated by loneliness or the desire for more positive and fulfilling friendships, it is important to practise self-love first.

Write down mantras that reinforce your self-confidence to remind your subconscious that you have something important and interesting to offer in new interactions. Rather than feeding the doubts that have been standing in your way, you could say:
"I am fun", "I am confident", "I am likeable".

Practise your chosen mantras at the same times every day using the 369 Numerology Method (see page 36) to reinforce them. Once you start to believe these truths, you will radiate these qualities when you meet new people and welcome new connections into your life.

MANIFEST DREAMS

Romantic love

If you're searching for your soulmate, manifestation can't attract a Hollywood heartthrob to your local speed dating event, but it might help you send out the right vibrations to the people around you.

LOVE & RELATIONSHIPS

A static picture of your future partner might not be enough here and, in fact, defining them in too much detail, such as their eye colour or exact height, could be holding you back. Try creating a more dynamic vision of a future together by attaching strong, tangible feelings to your intention.

MANIFEST DREAMS

Attracting love

Find a silent, private space where you can light a candle with a romantic, floral scent. Conjuring up feelings of excitement, anticipation and optimism will raise your positive vibrations and therefore the energy you can attract. Try listening to a love song at a soothing volume and repeat a series of affirmations about your future romance.
You might say:

LOVE & RELATIONSHIPS

> "I am in a passionate relationship that makes me feel fulfilled, happy and safe. My partner and I love movie nights at home, cooking adventurous dishes together and taking last-minute holidays to places we have never explored. This love is cosy and thrilling at the same time. Like butterflies fluttering in my stomach."

> **"To acquire love… fill yourself up with it until you become a magnet."**

Charles F. Haanel,
The Master Key System (1916)

LOVE & RELATIONSHIPS

Deeper connections

What if you have had love and lost it: can manifestation help you attract more love to a marriage or another existing relationship? Certainly, fixating on your negative emotions can be defeatist and signal to the universe that you have given up – or that someone has given up on you. Your actions might therefore be conflicting with your loving desires.

Joyful memories are a powerful way to tap into loving feelings and more likely to remind you to act on your relationship in a giving way, with communication and compassion.

You could spend as little as 68 seconds a day tapping into the best feelings of love you can remember in order to positively shift the vibrations you send out. Look at old photos, watch holiday videos and read back loving messages. You will radiate love and positive energy within minutes.

Starting a family

Belief is an integral part of the manifestation equation. While you might willingly "ask" the universe for a baby, it is harder to have faith that if you continue to "believe" you will "receive", especially when certain challenges are sent your way. However, positive affirmations have a tremendous power to focus the mind on "when" a positive outcome will happen, rather than harbouring doubt about "if".

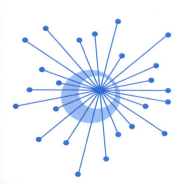

LOVE & RELATIONSHIPS

It is not enough to tell yourself: "My baby will come when the time is right" unless you firmly trust that the universe will deliver.

To clear the path to your desired outcome, identify and remove any obstacles. Are you holding onto envy or resentment? Can you let go of frustration or doubt? It is this release that helps to trust in the process of manifestation.

"Only one person can be in charge of your joy, of your bliss, and that's you. So even your parent, your child, your spouse – they don't have the control to create your happiness. They simply have the opportunity to share in your happiness."

Lisa Nichols, *The Secret* (2006)

LOVE & RELATIONSHIPS

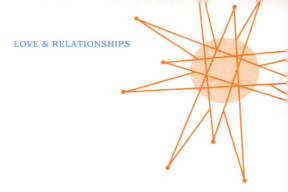

Repairing relationships

In families, as in friendships, there are always highs and lows. For healthier connections, work through any sadness, guilt or judgement with positivity for what your relationship could be.

MANIFEST DREAMS

Write a letter

To repair a relationship, take pen to paper and replace any negativity you currently feel with optimism. Write a letter to yourself from the future, describing the joy that reconnecting with this individual has brought to your life, being clear about how it has improved your wellbeing. Talk in detail about the successful actions you took, which have led to the fulfilling experiences you have shared together since.

LOVE & RELATIONSHIPS

Writing in the present tense not only encourages your brain to deeply experience these emotions and associate them with your friend or family member, it will shift your attention away from how you originally reached a bad place in the relationship.

Knowing when to let go

There is no place for toxicity in manifestation. Negative friends, family members or partners can drain what you have worked so hard to achieve. Protecting that energy is as important as seeking it out from the universe.

Toxicity could come in the form of insults that knock your self-confidence, undermining behaviour that damages your self-worth or gaslighting, which makes you constantly question yourself. All of these behaviours stop you from moving forward.

LOVE & RELATIONSHIPS

Setting boundaries

Distancing yourself from toxic bonds opens space for new connections that build up your vibrations. It's not always easy (or even possible) to completely sever relationships, but setting your boundaries could help.

If a family member consistently brings you down, face them on a day when you feel strong enough to deflect it. Perhaps you have to remain friends with your ex for the sake of your family. Insecurity and regret about the failure of that relationship could block new love, whereas affirmations of self-worth will attract someone worthy of you.

Releasing toxic people

Setting an intention to not react or respond to any toxicity is a great starting point for releasing the bond, but here are some specific tips.

1 Tell them how you feel
This is for you, not for them. It allows you to put your intention into words and actions.

2 Distance yourself physically and emotionally
Unfollow them on social media, say no to get-togethers, cancel plans.

3 Keep your boundaries sacred
If you find it hard to remain strong and keep getting pulled into their orbit, set a no-contact, no-response rule for a short period of time, and then keep extending it.

4 Forgive and let go
This doesn't mean forgetting how the relationship has hurt you or that you are giving them another chance. It means you are releasing them from your life.

LOVE & RELATIONSHIPS

5 ways to feel the love

1 Watch a romantic comedy: Laughter and love are a strong combination.

2 Have a cuddle: Hugs and kisses release the love hormone oxytocin.

3 Pay yourself a compliment: Treat yourself the way you want to be treated.

4 Put yourself first: You can't give unless you have enough to share.

5 Do something you love: Whether it's a walk or a bubble bath.

Chapter Four

HEALING & EMOTIONS

MANIFEST DREAMS

If manifestation can deliver abundance, can it also help you to overcome adversity? When all else has failed, the healing power and spiritual enlightenment of manifestation is one of the most common reasons people turn to this remarkable practice. Finding your power to bounce back can bring light, even in the darkest times.

> "We are never more than a belief away from our greatest love, deepest healing and most profound miracles."

Gregg Braden, *The Spontaneous Healing of Belief* (2006)

Tools for emotional healing

Crystals. Some people believe they amplify our energy and aid in physical and emotional healing.

Candles. Scents tap into our emotion centres.

Music. Soothing sounds can focus our minds.

Notebook. Draw, write or doodle your desires.

Sage. Burning a bundle of sage, known as smudging, is a spiritual ritual to combat negative energy.

Recordings. Tape, listen and repeat personalized mantras and affirmations.

HEALING & EMOTIONS

Serenity

Practise mindfulness in the moments where you catch your thoughts running too far ahead. One of the biggest causes of stress in our lives is the compounding worry about what is coming next: in an hour's time, in the next week, over the coming months. You cannot live in the current moment if you are rushing straight to the next. Instead, focusing your thoughts on one moment at a time feels more peaceful and manageable.

MANIFEST DREAMS

Morning meditation

Start with your morning coffee and make yourself 100 per cent present in the process of preparing it and enjoying it. Turn off the radio, close the kitchen door and create silence. Choose a cup that brings you joy.

HEALING & EMOTIONS

Is there an inscription, a texture or a colour that feels familiar when you see it in the cupboard?

Notice the splash of the milk as you pour it into your tea or coffee or as you froth it.

Breathe in. How satisfying does the hot drink smell as you make it and what feelings does it bring up for you?

Pause and then taste. What does that first sip feel like: from the texture, to the flavour and the familiar rush of energy.

A moment of mindfulness as simple (and seemingly insignificant) as this will prime your mind for productivity and create space for important thoughts, instead of attracting more stress.

Fitness goals

Clear intentions and positive mantras make a powerful combination for manifesting better physical health. Athletes like Simone Biles and Michael Phelps have taught us that training is as much about what the mind believes is possible as what our bodies are capable of.

However, the temptation with goal-setting in fitness is to negatively fixate on what you don't have (like a six-pack). Thinking about the absence of something makes it seem out of reach and therefore any desire to work at it feels futile. Powerful intentions that talk directly to your subconscious in the present tense encourage you to act more consistently on these goals and seek out opportunities to make them a reality, because you make yourself believe the goal is possible.

"I make time to train my body."

"I lift heavy weights because I am stronger than yesterday."

"My body has all of the oxygen it needs to push myself."

Train the mind & body

Whenever you train your body, you can be training your mind with mantras. Telling yourself: "I can't do this" gives your mind the signal to stop your legs, put the weights down, take a seat and catch your breath. Whereas, reciting a mantra is the start of progress that uses your thought to change your actions in pursuit of your desired outcome.

For example, if you say "I am strong, I am fit, I am fast", your mind will tell your body: "I can do this", "I can run faster", "I can push harder", "I can finish this".

> **The law of attraction says that like attracts like, and when you think and feel what you want to attract on the inside, the law will use people, circumstances and events to magnetize what you want.**

Rhonda Byrne, *The Secret* (2006)

MANIFEST DREAMS

Emotional healing

Manifestation can't stop bad things from happening, but it can change how you react to them. You have the power to turn a negative into a positive by manifesting resilience in your life. And while healing from traumatic events is best achieved with professional help, spiritual enlightenment will encourage you to trust that the universe has your back.

By the law of attraction, if we respond to negative events with pessimism and self-loathing, we will attract further negativity into our lives. On the other hand, learning to let go of negative thoughts, feelings and beliefs attracts positive, healing energy.

Effective manifestation is not about ignoring negative feelings. Actually, acknowledging and then releasing them can be cathartic. Journal your emotions, but instead of fixating on disappointment, show acceptance for the events; this encourages hope for change.

Physical healing

When we think about illness and suffering, we are drawing more negativity into our bodies with our thoughts. Manifesting physical healing requires a shift in our energy to a hopeful, higher energy, which – if you can't draw it in for yourself – can sometimes be drawn from nature.

The Ancient Greeks used water to treat everything from back injuries to open wounds, believing that this contact with the natural world had unique healing properties. When you immerse yourself in water (even if it is just your hands) not only can you start to calm your thoughts to a state of mindfulness but the sensory experience of temperature, touch and sound can interrupt any feelings of pain and discomfort. This focused, peaceful state can help raise your vibrations.

HEALING & EMOTIONS

Sleep on it

Meditation is not only used to manifest better sleep but to continue manifesting while you sleep. The two processes go hand in hand: the assumption being that if you can master meditation, you can sleep peacefully and dream big!

Many people who experience insomnia describe their minds as racing late at night. Meditative practice helps to clear unwelcome thoughts and, when accompanied by visualization, can prime the subconscious to focus on relaxing images as you drift off to sleep.

Sleep wind-down

Start by creating a peaceful environment. Combine low lighting with soothing music and privacy. Scan your body, noticing where you feel any tension. Your bed should be a naturally comfortable space but a supportive head pillow and soft, freshly washed sheets intensify the experience.

By now, you should be able to concentrate fully on your breathing to help clear your mind and, if you're not already drifting off into a deep slumber, this is the perfect starting point for your manifestation practice.

HEALING & EMOTIONS

478 breathing

This breathing pattern aims to reduce anxiety and help you get to sleep, and can be a good way to ground yourself before setting an intention or repeating a mantra. A form of breath regulation called pranayama, it helps you avoid intrusive thoughts or worries by concentrating your mind on repeating the pattern.

Take a deep inhale for 4 seconds, hold the breath for 7 seconds and exhale for 8 seconds. Repeat.

MANIFEST DREAMS

Box breathing visualization

Try this simple breathwork technique for deeper manifestation.

1 Sit quietly and comfortably with the eyes closed. Slowly breathe in four a count of four.

2 Hold your breath for 4 seconds.

3 Slowly exhale for 4 seconds.

4 Repeat steps 1 to 3 until you feel centred.

Overcoming fears

Identify what is standing between you and your goals. It could be the theoretical fear of failure or a fear of letting go. Fear might otherwise present itself as a tangible phobia of flying that's stopping you from manifesting your dream holiday. Whatever fear is holding you back, manifestation cannot take hold until you address it.

Fear, worry, anxiety and sadness are all emotions that are associated with low energy. Until you raise the vibrations of these feelings, you cannot attract positive outcomes.

HEALING & EMOTIONS

Letting go of fears

To truly open up to potential, let go of the limiting self-beliefs that hold you back, such as fear of failure, imposter syndrome and poor self-worth. You have just as much right to everything the world offers as anyone else.

1 Challenge your thoughts and how these relate to your core self beliefs – do they logically make sense to you or do the facts say otherwise?

2 Don't compare yourself to others – you will automatically find some fault within yourself.

3 Stop fighting your feelings – lean into them and accept them.

4 Understand that fear is a perception of the mind only and negative outcomes can be perceived as the universe directing you elsewhere.

5 Do what you want, what aligns with your beliefs, not what anyone else wants or believes.

Keep a positivity journal

To raise your vibrations, keep a daily positivity journal to reflect on great things that happened. While fear often manifests itself in thoughts about the future and something you are dreading, this exercise gives your mind a chance to recognize and celebrate all of the successes you might have had in the face of dread, anxiety or worry. You are training your subconscious to believe that you can achieve, which will gradually reflect on the way you approach each new day.

> **"You are the master of your destiny. You can influence, direct and control your own environment. You can make your life what you want it to be."**
>
> Napoleon Hill,
> *Think and Grow Rich* (1937)

CONCLUSION

It's time to stop dreaming and manifest your best life. You have the knowledge, the tools and, hopefully, the belief that things can really start happening for you. Now all that is left is to take actions to turn your thoughts and feelings into the future you have dreamed of.

Ready to manifest a reality? Let's make it happen.

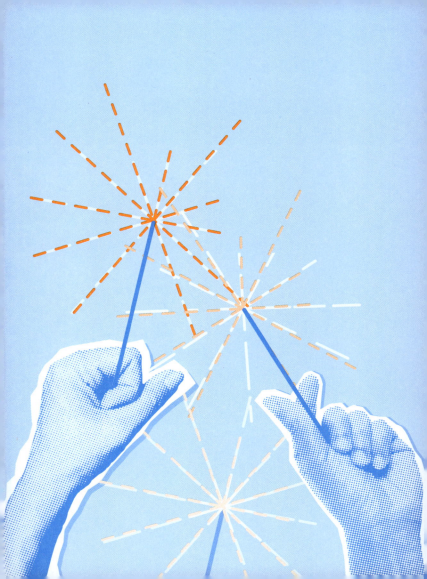

FURTHER READING

Julia Cameron, *The Artist's Way: A Spiritual Path to Higher Creativity*, Souvenir Press, 2020.

Jordanna Levin, *Make It Happen: Manifest the Life of Your Dreams*, Murdoch Books, 2021.

Roxie Nafousi, *Manifest: 7 Steps to Living Your Best Life*, Penguin Michael Joseph, 2022.

Rhonda Byrne, *The Secret* (10th Anniversary Edition), Simon & Schuster, 2016.

WEBSITES

medium.com/@roamingyogi/manifesting-through-the-chakras-moving-down-the-manifestation-current-17c4fae9f0b1

medium.com/@deborahbranco_55867/how-to-set-clear-and-powerful-intentions-for-manifestation-the-ultimate-guide-9cd579737bdc

medium.com/@pbswope111/68-second-mantra-for-creating-a-lifechanging-manifestation-a0b00c163aae